American Edu
Research Association

Prevention of Bullying in Schools, Colleges, and Universities

Research Report and Recommendations

AMERICAN
EDUCATIONAL
RESEARCH
ASSOCIATION

2013
Washington, DC
www.aera.net

American Educational Research Association
1430 K Street, NW
Suite 1200
Washington, DC 20005

Notice: This report was prepared under the auspices of the AERA Council, the governing body of the Association, using only funds provided by the Association. Members of the AERA Task Force responsible for preparation of the report were selected for their special competencies and with regard to appropriate balance. All Task Force members are members of AERA, and all served without compensation.

This report was adopted by the AERA Council in February 2013.

ISBN 978-0-935302-37-0

Additional copies of this report, including an electronic version, are available from the American Educational Research Association at http://www.aera.net.

Cover design by Anna Rosich
Printed in the United States of America

Suggested citation: American Educational Research Association. (2013). *Prevention of bullying in schools, colleges, and universities: Research report and recommendations*. Washington, DC: American Educational Research Association.

American Educational Research Association

The American Educational Research Association (AERA) is the national interdisciplinary research association for approximately 25,000 scholars who undertake research on education and learning. Founded in 1916, AERA aims to advance knowledge about education, to encourage scholarly inquiry related to education, and to promote the use of research to improve education and serve the public good. AERA is dedicated to strengthening education research by promoting research of the highest quality, undertaking education and training programs, and advancing sound research and science policy. The Association publishes six peer-reviewed journals and research and methodology books central to the field. It also offers courses, small grants, and dissertation and postdoctoral training initiatives supported by federal research agencies and private foundations.

American Educational Research Association
Task Force on the Prevention of
Bullying in Schools, Colleges, and Universities

Dorothy L. Espelage (Co-Chair), University of Illinois, Urbana-Champaign

Ron Avi Astor (Co-Chair), University of Southern California

Dewey Cornell, University of Virginia

Jaime Lester, George Mason University

Matthew J. Mayer, Rutgers University

Elizabeth J. Meyer, California Polytechnic State University

V. Paul Poteat, Boston College

Brendesha Tynes, University of Southern California

American Educational Research Association Council
2012–2013

Contents

Introduction

Bullying presents one of the greatest health risks to children, youth, and young adults in U.S. society. It is pernicious in its impact even if often less visible and less readily identifiable than other public health concerns. Its effects on victims, perpetrators, and even bystanders are both immediate and long term and can affect the development and functioning of individuals across generations.

The epicenter for bullying is schools, colleges, and universities, where vast numbers of children, youth, and young adults spend much of their time. Bullying—a form of harassment and violence—should be examined from a developmental, social, and educational perspective. The educational settings in which it occurs and where prevention and intervention are possible need to be understood as potential contexts for positive change. Yet many administrators, teachers, and related personnel lack training to address bullying and do not know how to intervene to reduce it.[1]

These circumstances drove the decision by the American Educational Research Association (AERA) to undertake this report. As a scientific association, AERA seeks to bring research to bear on significant issues related to education, teaching, and learning. In addition to encouraging scholarship in

---

1. This point was set forth as part of the original charge to the Task Force crafted by William G. Tierney, 2012–2013 AERA President.

the field and supporting its wide dissemination, AERA pursues projects to make research accessible on issues vital to the public good. This report is one example.

Background of This Report

Prevention of Bullying in Schools, Colleges, and Universities continues a line of research led by AERA to address challenging issues in human behavior, development, and interaction in educational environments. In 2010, AERA published a special issue of the *Educational Researcher* titled "New Perspectives on School Safety and Violence Prevention" and held a Capitol Hill briefing on the subject. Also in 2010, AERA created an online research bibliography on lesbian, gay, bisexual, transgendered, queer (LGBTQ) issues in education and held an intensive research workshop on the topic, bringing together diverse scholars in the field. A major volume representing the state of the knowledge on LGBTQ issues and research needs and directions will be published in 2013.

In February 2012, at the recommendation of AERA's then president-elect William G. Tierney, the AERA Council established a Task Force on the Prevention of Bullying in Schools, Colleges, and Universities.[2] Comprising a small group of diverse experts, the Task Force examined the state of the research knowledge about bullying across K–16 and addressed implications for practice and policy aimed at evidence-based prevention. The AERA Task Force differed from others that have focused on psychological skills, psychological processes, and program interventions; instead, it focused on the social context of bullying in educational settings. This Task Force was also unique in examining bullying research and potential interventions as they relate to school reform, teacher education, administrator education, special education, and cultural

---

2. Special acknowledgement is due to 2012–2013 President Tierney, Task Force Co-Chairs Dorothy Espelage and Ron Astor, and the entire Task Force for their commitment to this effort and for effectively defining the scope of the work and accomplishing it in less than one year.

diversity in postsecondary schools, departments, and programs of education.

The Task Force Charge

The mandate of the Task Force was to prepare and present to the AERA Council practical short-term and long-term recommendations to address bullying among children, youth, and young adults. The goal was to develop research-based recommendations for ensuring safe, respectful, and productive educational environments, where optimal learning can occur and where individuals take responsibility for their own behavior and its impact on others. Accordingly, the Task Force received the following charge:

(1) To identify the causes and consequences of bullying in schools, colleges, and universities;

(2) To highlight training and technical assistance opportunities so that faculty and staff at all types of educational institutions may effectively address bullying;

(3) To evaluate the effectiveness of current anti-bullying policies and bullying prevention programs; and

(4) To assess the connections between bullying research and interventions and current and pending legislation.

Preparation, Review, and Adoption of the Report

The Task Force identified key issues and responded to the charge by developing a series of accessible research briefs that focus on practical strategies and policies while providing access to the underlying scientific, peer-reviewed studies and related books and reports that were foundational to the recommendations. The briefs are not intended to be an exhaustive review of the research literature but rather to capture the state of the research knowledge, translate empirical findings for diverse audiences of users, and identify gaps in research and data that need to be addressed to best serve policy and practice in the future.

Members of the Task Force took the lead in preparing these briefs based on their expertise. All members, and in particular the co-chairs, provided critique and comment on each brief and on the entire set of briefs. Prior to completion, the briefs were reviewed favorably by an independent peer group of experts.[3] There were then final revisions based on feedback.

In February 2013, the AERA Council reviewed the report and unanimously approved its adoption and wide dissemination to relevant communities engaged in addressing bullying or charting the course of prevention programs, professional development, or research investment in education at all levels.

Format of the Report

The report is presented as a series of 11 briefs. All but one present research and set forth conclusions and implications.[4] In offering short and accessible briefs, AERA intends to provide an overview of the knowledge that can be relied on and to signal to those in policy and practice this association's commitment to working with knowledge users and producers in the prevention of bullying in our schools, colleges, and universities.

Felice J. Levine
AERA Executive Director

---

3. AERA wishes to thank Rami Benbenishty, Bar-Ilan University; Michael J. Furlong, University of California, Santa Barbara; Nancy G. Guerra, University of Delaware; Etta Hollins, University of Missouri, Kansas City; Cynthia Hudley, University of California, Santa Barbara; and Robert S. Rueda, University of Southern California, for serving as a review group for the draft bullying briefs.

4. Brief 9, "Using Evidence-Based Programs in Schools to Take on Bullying," focuses entirely on applications that follow from the research.

Brief 1

Looking Beyond the Traditional
Definition of Bullying

Bullying is a highly varied form of aggression where there is systematic use and abuse of power. Bullying can include physical aggression such as hitting and shoving, and verbal aggression, such as name-calling (Espelage, 2012; Vaillancourt et al., 2008). It can also include social or relational forms of bullying in which a victim is excluded by peers or subjected to humiliation. Bullying can occur face-to-face or through digital media such as text messages, social media, and websites. There are mild, moderate, and severe levels of bullying.

Definitions of Bullying

Traditionally, bullying has been defined as:

- Unwanted, intentional, aggressive behavior that involves a real or perceived power imbalance that is often repeated over time (Olweus, 1993).

- Actions of verbal and physical aggression that range in severity from making threats and spreading rumors to isolating or excluding others, to physical attacks causing injury. The formal definition of bullying includes all behaviors that fit the stated criteria. Therefore, even severe acts involving weapon use, gang activity, or crimes could fit the formal definition of bullying if they

Task Force members Dorothy L. Espelage and Ron Avi Astor took the lead in drafting this brief.

involve a power imbalance. Some researchers include these behaviors and some do not.

With few exceptions, researchers *have not* used the traditional definition. Instead, they have proceeded in various ways:

- Some researchers provide students with the traditional definition and then assess prevalence in small (not representative) samples. This practice ignores research showing that the use of a definition influences prevalence rates, and it does not consider findings that youth identify bullying with these components (Vaillancourt et al., 2008).

- National epidemiological studies provide a definition and simply ask students if they have been bullied or if they have bullied another student within a specific time frame provided. For example, the Centers for Disease Control and Prevention (2012) assessed two items of lifetime victimization (bullied on school property and bullied electronically; see http://www.cdc.gov/). Similarly, Nansel, Overpeck, Pilla, Ruan, Simons-Morton, and Scheidt (2001) assessed victimization or perpetration at school or away from school since last term/semester with a total of four items.

- Other researchers simply provide youth with a list of behavioral descriptors of aggressive behaviors (e.g., name-calling, hitting, excluding), assess frequency within a specific time frame, and sum these experiences. Higher scores on these victimization and perpetration scales are considered a marker of severity, and the scales are used to study predictors of the phenomena, but no direct assessment of intentionality or power differential is assessed (Espelage, Holt, & Henkel, 2003; Espelage, Basile, & Hamburger, 2012; Espelage, Green, & Polanin, 2012).

- Researchers typically assume intentionality, equate frequency reflecting the actions of many students with repetition from the same bully, and rarely assess the power imbalance directly (for an exception, see Rodkin, Espelage, & Hanish, in press). Some have argued that repetition is an index of severity but does not define bullying (Rodkin et al., in press).

Some bullying behaviors may overlap with aggression that meets the legal definition of harassment, assault, or school crime, but not all incidents of harassment or assault are bullying. Without the components of intentionality, repetition, and power combined in the behavior of the same person, bullying victimization is the same as school victimization.

Conclusions and Implications

Bullying is part of the larger phenomenon of violence in schools and communities. Educators and scholars should not limit themselves to the traditional definition. Since it is not fully clear to what extent victimization and bullying overlap, the public and researchers should assess both victimization and bullying behaviors. Further, the examination of victimization should involve interactions among all community members, including youth, teachers, school staff, parents, and so forth. As a result of differences in definition, there is no consensus on the incidence of bullying or on trends over time. There is a need for researchers to agree upon how best to define and measure bullying and to reach consensus on comparable use. Research that distinguishes more carefully among types of bullying and levels of severity would make it possible to monitor levels of bullying and evaluate intervention efforts in a more standardized manner.

References

Centers for Disease Control and Prevention. (2012). Youth Risk Behavior Surveillance—United States, 2011. *MMWR, 61* (No. SS-04), 1–162.

Espelage, D. L. (2012). Bullying prevention: A research dialogue with Dorothy Espelage. *Prevention Researcher, 19*(3), 17–19.

Espelage, D. L., Basile, K. C., & Hamburger, M. E. (2012). Bullying experiences and co-occurring sexual violence perpetration among middle school students: Shared and unique risk factors. *Journal of Adolescent Health, 50,* 60–65.

Espelage, D. L., Green, H. D., & Polanin, J. (2012). Willingness to intervene in bullying episodes among middle school students: Individual and peer-group influences. *Journal of Early Adolescence, 32,* 776–801.

Espelage, D. L., Holt, M. K., & Henkel, R. R. (2003). Examination of peer-group contextual effects on aggression during early adolescence. *Child Development, 74,* 205–220.

Nansel, T. R., Overpeck, M. D., Pilla, R. S., Ruan, W. J., Simons-Morton, B., & Scheidt, P. (2001). Bullying behaviors among US youth: Prevalence and association with psychosocial adjustment. *Journal of the American Medical Association, 16,* 2094–2100.

Olweus, D. (1993). *Bullying at school.* Oxford, UK: Blackwell.

Rodkin, P. C., Espelage, D. L., & Hanish, L. D. (in press). A relational perspective on the social ecology of bullying. *American Psychologist.*

Vaillancourt, T., McDougall, P., Hymel, S., Krygsman, A., Miller, J., Stiver, K., & Davis, C. (2008). Bullying: Are researchers and children/youth talking about the same thing? *International Journal of Behavioral Development, 32*(6), 486–495.

Brief 2

Bullying as a Pervasive Problem

Bullying is pervasive in all grades and all schools nationwide. It is observed across gender, race, ethnicity, and socioeconomic status. The percentages of students involved in bullying vary widely according to the definition of bullying that is used; however, one nationally representative survey found that approximately 28% of students ages 12 to 18 reported being bullied at school during the school year (Robers, Zhang, Truman, & Snyder, 2012). Other studies have found comparably high percentages of students who admit bullying their peers (Wang, Iannotti, & Nansel, 2009). When the impact of bullying on bystanders is considered along with the impact on victims and aggressors, it is likely that bullying affects most students at some time during a typical school year.

Measurable Negative Consequences of Bullying

- Bullied students experience higher rates of anxiety, depression, physical health problems, and social adjustment problems. These problems can persist into adulthood (Carlisle & Rofes, 2007; Espelage, Low, & De La Rue, 2012; Gini & Pozzoli, 2009; Ttofi, Farrington, Lösel, & Loeber, 2011).

Task Force members Dewey Cornell, Dorothy L. Espelage, Matthew J. Mayer, Brendesha Tynes, and Ron Avi Astor took the lead in drafting this brief.

- Bullying students become less engaged in school, and their grades and test scores decline (Cornell, Gregory, Huang, & Fan, 2013; Juvonen, Wang, & Espinoza, 2011; Robers et al., 2012).

- In high schools where bullying and teasing are prevalent, the student body is less involved in school activities, performs lower on standardized tests, and has a lower graduation rate (Espelage & De La Rue, in press; Mehta, Cornell, Fan, & Gregory, in press).

- Students who engage in bullying are at elevated risk for poor school adjustment and delinquency. They are at increased risk for higher rates of criminal behavior and social maladjustment in adulthood (Bender & Lösel, 2011; Farrington & Ttofi, 2011).

- Students who are bullied but also engage in bullying have more negative outcomes than students in bully-only or victim-only groups (Espelage & De La Rue, in press; Ttofi et al., 2011).

- Cyberbullying has become more prevalent and raises concern because of its potential for widespread dissemination and intensified humiliation of targeted students. On average, a large proportion of students say they have been cyberbullied in their lifetimes. Rates can vary widely depending on the time frame and type of study (Schneider, O'Donnell, Stueve, & Coulter, 2012; Tokunaga, 2010; Wade & Beran, 2011; Wang et al., 2009).

- Cyberbullied students experience negative outcomes similar to those experienced by their traditional counterparts, including depression, poor academic performance, and problem behavior. Cyber-victimization is also linked to suicidal ideation, and students with these thoughts are more likely to attempt suicide (Hinduja & Patchin, 2010; Tokunaga, 2010).

Victimization Trends and the Inclusion of Other School Violence Indicators

Monitoring of trends in victimization needs to include other school violence indicators (Robers et al., 2012). Examining total victimization on school grounds, including physical violence and serious physical violence, reveals that between 1995 and 2009 there has been more than a 50% reduction for student groups across gender and age and in public and private schools. Even with these national reductions over-all, some forms of violent victimization on school grounds have not changed over time. For example, the percentage of students being threatened by a weapon on school grounds remained fairly stable during this period—between 7% and 9%—whereas the percentage of students in Grades 9–12 who reported being in a physical fight decreased from 16% to 11% between 1993 and 2009.

Bullying may encompass these forms of violence but also extends to a wide array of behaviors that include social exclusion, cyber bullying, verbal hate language, and public humiliation. In 2009, about 28% of U.S. students aged 12–18 reported being bullied at school during the school year. However, the rates of bullying vary widely by type of bullying behavior, by region, and by age, gender, and ethnicity. Therefore, accurate epidemiological estimates require that each type of bullying behavior be carefully examined within each age, geographic, and behavioral context.

Conclusions and Implications

Bullying embraces a range of behaviors that vary in type and severity. It is difficult to reach a consensus on the incidence of bullying or trends over time because of both the variability in how bullying is defined across studies and the broad classification of bullying behavior, with little disaggregation by the nature of the incident or the use of power by the perpetrator(s). Research that distinguishes more carefully between different types of bullying, types of co-occurrence with other forms of school violence, and levels of severity would improve the assessment of bullying and general victimization rates and improve the sensitivity of measures of effects of intervention efforts.

References

Bender, D., & Lösel, F. (2011). Bullying at school as a predictor of delinquency, violence and other anti-social behaviour in adulthood. *Criminal Behaviour and Mental Health, 21*, 99–106. doi:10.1002/cbm.799

Carlisle, N., & Rofes, E. (2007). School bullying: Do adult survivors perceive long-term effects? *Traumatology, 13*(1), 16–26.

Cornell, D., Gregory, A., Huang, F., & Fan, X. (2013). Perceived prevalence of teasing and bullying predicts high school dropout rates. *Journal of Educational Psychology, 105*(1), 138–149. doi:10.1037/a0030416

Espelage, D. L. & De La Rue, L. (in press). School bullying: Its nature and ecology. *International Journal of Adolescent Medicine and Health.*

Espelage, D. L., Low, S., & De La Rue, L. (2012). Relations between peer victimization subtypes, family violence, and psychological outcomes during adolescence. *Psychology of Violence, 2*(4), 313–324. doi:10.1037/a0027386

Farrington, D. P., & Ttofi, M. M. (2011). Bullying as a predictor of offending, violence and later life outcomes. *Criminal Behaviour and Mental Health, 21*(2), 90–98. doi:10.1002/cbm.801

Gini, G., & Pozzoli, T. (2009). Association between bullying and psychosomatic problems: A meta analysis. *Pediatrics, 123*, 1059–1065.

Hinduja, S., & Patchin, J. (2010). Bullying, cyberbullying and suicide. *Archives of Suicidal Research, 14*, 206–221.

Juvonen, J., Wang, Y., & Espinoza, G. (2011). Bullying experiences and compromised academic performance across middle school grades. *Journal of Early Adolescence, 31*, 152–173.

Mehta, S., Cornell, D., Fan, X., & Gregory, A. (in press). Bullying climate and school engagement in ninth-grade students. *Journal of School Health.*

Robers, S., Zhang, J., Truman, J., & Snyder, T. (2012). *Indicators of school crime and safety: 2011* (NCES 2012-002/NCJ 236021). Washington, DC: National Center for Education Statistics, U.S. Department of Education, and Bureau of Justice Statistics, Office of Justice Programs, U.S. Department of Justice.

Schneider, S. K., O'Donnell, L., Stueve, A., & Coulter, R. (2012). Cyberbullying, school bullying, and psychological distress: A regional census of high school students. *American Journal of Public Health, 102*, 171–177.

Tokunaga, R. S. (2010). Following you home from school: A critical review and synthesis of research on cyberbullying victimization. *Computers in Human Behavior, 26*, 277–287.

Ttofi, M. M., Farrington, D. P., Lösel, F., & Loeber, R. (2011). Do the victims of school bullies tend to become depressed later in life? A systematic review and meta-analysis of longitudinal studies. *Journal of Aggression, Conflict and Peace Research, 3*, 63–73.

Wade, A., & Beran, T. (2011). Cyberbullying: The new era of bullying. *Canadian Journal of School Psychology, 26*, 44–61.

Wang, J., Iannotti, R., & Nansel, T. (2009). School bullying among adolescents in the United States: Physical, verbal, relational, and cyber. *Journal of Adolescent Health, 45*, 368–375.

Brief 3

Bullying and Peer Victimization Among Vulnerable Populations

Research on bullying dynamics shows that bullying is often aimed at specific groups. Findings from three groups have become prominent in the research literature: children with disabilities, African American youth, and LGBTQ youth. Historically, the research literature has omitted, distorted, or underresearched these three populations. There needs to be much more investment in research that examines the unique bullying dynamics surrounding vulnerable populations.

Bullying Among Students With Disabilities

Overall Prevalence of Bullying Among Students With Disabilities

- Students with disabilities are twice as likely to be identified as perpetrators and victims as are students without disabilities (Rose, Espelage, Aragon, & Elliott, 2011; Rose & Espelage, 2012).

- Students with disabilities that are characterized by, or have diagnostic criteria associated with, low social skills and low communication skills have a higher likelihood of involvement in bullying incidents (Rose, Monda-Amaya, & Espelage, 2011).

Task Force members Dorothy L. Espelage and Brendesha Tynes took the lead in drafting this brief.

- A meta-analysis of 152 studies found that 8 of 10 children with a learning disability (LD) were peer-rated as rejected; that 8 of 10 were rated as deficient in social competence and social problem solving; and that LD students were less often selected as friends by their peers (Baumeister, Storch, & Geffken, 2008).

The Importance of Type of Disability in Bullying

- Recent empirical investigations suggest that victimization may be predicted by the severity of the disability (Rose, 2010).

- For example, students with autism may be victimized more (Bejerot & Mörtberg, 2009), and students with learning disabilities may be victimized less, than other subgroups of students with disabilities (Wallace, Anderson, Bartholomay, & Hupp, 2002; White & Loeber, 2008).

- Unfortunately, much of the extant literature varies on victimization rates of individual subgroups of students with disabilities, making direct subgroup comparisons difficult (Rose, 2010).

African Americans in Bullying, Victimization, and Harassment Research

Prevalence Rates and Measurement Issues for African American Youth

- Research indicates that prevalence rates of bullying victimization vary considerably for African American youth based on the wording in measures. For example, both girls and middle school boys who are African American may report being a victim with behavior-based measures (including various types of bullying

behaviors), but may be less likely to report that these experiences are frequent with definition-based measures
(Sawyer, Bradshaw, & O'Brennan, 2008). This suggests
that African American youth may have differing con-
ceptions of bullying victimization and therefore may
underreport their victimization experiences.

- When considering six types of victimization in school
  and neighborhood contexts, including peer physical
  assault (being hit, kicked, punched, or attacked with
  or without a weapon), physical intimidation (being
  grabbed, chased, or forced to do something against one's
  will), and relational victimization, researchers found
  that African American youth experience *more* physical assaults than their White and Latino counterparts
  (31.5% as opposed to 20.7% and 19.1%, respectively)
  (Turner, Finkelhor, Hamby, Shattuck, & Ormrod, 2011).
  Although most of these incidents occur in school, 41.5%
  of assaults in the sample occurred outside of school.

- With regard to bullying and harassment perpetration,
  several reports show that African American youth are
  overrepresented (Carlyle & Steinman, 2007; Espelage,
  Basile, & Hamburger, 2012; Low & Espelage, 2012).
  However, these reports utilize race-comparative designs
  that may privilege one cultural perspective over another
  and often yield small effect sizes between groups. In a
  study using a sample that included 100% African American youth, bullying perpetration rates were similar to
  those found in nationally representative samples (Fitzpatrick, Dulin, & Piko, 2010).

- Measurement concerns similar to those found in victimization research have emerged in studies of bullying
  perpetration. For example, when Carlyle and Steinman
  (2007) tested the validity of their bullying measures,
  they found the most inconsistencies in bullying classifi-

cation of African American youth and males. They also found that any racial differences in bullying perpetration disappear by 12th grade.

Outcomes Associated With Victimization and Harassment for African American Youth

- Victimization and harassment experiences are related to poorer social and emotional development, including depressive symptoms, greater difficulty making friends, poor relationships with classmates, peer rejection, negative self-appraisals, substance use, loneliness, below-average grades, and truancy (Cook, Williams, Guerra, Kim, & Sadek, 2010; Fitzpatrick et al., 2010; Nansel, Overpeck, Pilla, Ruan, Simons-Morton, & Scheidt, 2001; Russell, Sinclair, Poteat, & Koenig, 2012).

- In studies conducted in Wisconsin and California, the percentages of youth who reported harassment were 35.8% and 40.3%, respectively. Of the reported incidents, 15.8% in Wisconsin and 17.7% in California were race based. This is cause for concern as those who experience bias-based harassment have worse mental health status and substance use levels than those who experience non-bias-based harassment (Russell et al., 2012).

A growing body of literature documenting racial differences in bullying, victimization, and harassment points to an urgent need to better understand the experiences of African American youth. Findings from research on African American youth highlight a need for additional research, particularly related to the strengths (individual, cultural, and contextual) that youth possess that may buffer against the negative outcomes typically associated with bullying, victimization, and harassment. There is also a great need for researchers who are from diverse backgrounds and trained in African American youth culture and child development. Discrepancies in the literature highlight the fact that bullying, victimization, and harassment are major problems for this community and warrant culturally specific intervention and prevention strategies.

Bullying and the Lesbian, Gay, Bisexual (LGB) Community

*State of the Knowledge About Bullying
Among LGB Students*

- A large percentage of bullying among students involves the use of homophobic teasing and slurs (Espelage et al., 2012; Poteat & Espelage, 2005; Poteat & Rivers, 2010).

- Bullying and homophobic victimization occur more frequently among LGB youth in American schools than among students who identify as heterosexual (Espelage, Aragon, Birkett, & Koenig, 2008; Kosciw, Greytak, & Diaz, 2009).

- Some LGB youth report greater depression, anxiety, suicidal behaviors, and truancy than their straight-identified peers (Espelage et al., 2008; Robinson & Espelage, 2011).

- However, peer victimization does not appear to explain all of the mental health disparities between LGB and heterosexual youth (Robinson & Espelage, 2012).

*Effective Services and Programs for Preventing
and Intervening in Bullying for LGB Students*

Russell, Kosciw, Horn, and Saewyc (2010), in their *Social Policy Report* article "Safe Schools Policy for LGBTQ Students," highlight four practices that have been shown to promote safety and well-being for LGBTQ youth in schools:

- School nondiscrimination and anti-bullying policies that specifically include actual or perceived sexual orientation, gender identity, or expression (Russell & Mc-Guire, 2008)

- Teacher training and ongoing professional development on how to intervene when homophobic teasing occurs

- Presence of school-based support groups or clubs (e.g., gay-straight alliances)

- Inclusion of LGBTQ role models or issues in school curricula, including bullying-prevention programming and access to information and resources through the library, school-based health centers, and other sources

Conclusions and Implications

Research should be conducted to identify groups of individuals who are particularly vulnerable to bullying, harassment, and victimization, including individuals with disabilities, those who are gender-nonconforming or identify as LGBTQ, and African-American individuals. Although three groups are highlighted in this brief, research should include participants from other potentially vulnerable groups as well, including but not limited to those who identify as Native American, Latino/a, and/or Hispanic. Immigrant populations should also be included in future research studies. Race and ethnicity should be considered across class and socioeconomic status.

References

Baumeister, A. L., Storch, E. A., & Geffken, G. R. (2008). Peer victimization in children with learning disabilities. *Child and Adolescent Social Work Journal, 25,* 11–23. doi:10.1007/s10560-007-0109-6

Bejerot, S., & Mörtberg, E. (2009). Do autistic traits play a role in the bullying of obsessive compulsive disorder and social phobia sufferers? *Psychopathology, 42,* 170–176. doi:10.1159/000207459

Carlyle, K. E., & Steinman, K. J. (2007). Demographic differences in the prevalence, co-occurrence, and correlates of adolescent bullying at school. *Journal of School Health, 77*(9), 623–629.

Cook, C. R., Williams, K. R., Guerra, N. G., Kim, T. E., & Sadek, S. (2010). Predictors of bullying and victimization in childhood and adolescence: A meta-analytic investigation. *School Psychology Quarterly, 25*(2), 65–83.

Espelage, D. L., Aragon, S. R., Birkett, M., & Koenig, B. W. (2008). Homophobic teasing, psychological outcomes, and sexual orientation among high school students: What influences do parents and schools have? *School Psychology Review, 37,* 202–216.

Espelage, D. L., Basile, K. C., & Hamburger, M. E. (2012). Bullying experiences and co-occurring sexual violence perpetration among middle school students: Shared and unique risk factors. *Journal of Adolescent Health, 50,* 60–65.

Fitzpatrick, K., Dulin, A., & Piko, B. (2010). Bullying and depressive symptomatology among low-income African American youth. *Journal of Youth and Adolescence, 39,* 634–645.

Kosciw, J. G., Greytak, E. A., & Diaz, E. M. (2009). Who, what, when, where, and why: Demographic and ecological factors contributing to hostile school climate for lesbian, gay, bisexual, and transgender youth. *Journal of Youth and Adolescence, 38,* 976–988.

Low, S., & Espelage, D. (2012). Differentiating cyber bullying perpetration from non-physical bullying: Commonalities across race, individual, and family predictors. *Psychology of Violence, 3*(1), 39–52. doi:10.1037/a0030308

Nansel, T. R., Overpeck, M., Pilla, R. S., Ruan, W. J., Simons-Morton, B., & Scheidt, P. (2001). Bullying behaviors among US youth: Prevalence and association with psychosocial adjustment. *Journal of the American Medical Association, 285,* 2094–2100.

Poteat, V. P., & Espelage, D. L. (2005). Exploring the relation between bullying and homophobic verbal content: The Homophobic Content Agent Target (HCAT) scale. *Violence and Victims, 20,* 513–528.

Poteat, V. P., & Rivers, I. (2010). The use of homophobic language across bullying roles during adolescence. *Journal of Applied Developmental Psychology, 31*(2), 166–172.

Robinson, J. P., & Espelage, D. L. (2011). Inequities in educational and psychological outcomes between LGBTQ and straight students in middle and high school. *Educational Researcher, 40,* 315–330.

Robinson, J. P., & Espelage, D. L. (2012). Bullying explains only part of LGBTQ-heterosexual risk disparities: Implications for policy and practice. *Educational Researcher, 41*(8), 309–319.

Rose, C. A. (2010). Bullying among students with disabilities: Impact and implications. In D. L. Espelage & S. M. Swearer (Eds.), *Bullying in North American schools: A socio-ecological perspective on prevention and intervention* (2nd ed., pp. 34–44). Mahwah, NJ: Lawrence Erlbaum.

Rose, C. A., & Espelage, D. L. (2012). Risk and protective factors associated with the bullying involvement of students with emotional and behavioral disorders. *Behavioral Disorders, 37,* 133–148.

Rose, C. A., Espelage, D. L., Aragon, S. R., & Elliott, J. (2011). Bullying and victimization among students in special education and general education curricula. *Exceptionality Education International, 21*(2), 2–14.

Rose, C. A., Monda-Amaya, L. E., & Espelage, D. L. (2011). Bullying perpetration and victimization in special education: A review of the literature. *Remedial and Special Education, 32,* 114–130. doi:10.1177/0741932510361247

Russell, S. T., Kosciw, J. G., Horn, S. S., & Saewyc, E. (2010). Safe schools policy for LGBTQ Students. *Social Policy Report, 24*(4), 3–17. Washington DC: Society for Research in Child Development.

Russell, S., & McGuire, J. (2008). The school climate for lesbian, gay, bisexual, and transgender (LGBT) students. In M. Shinn & H. Yoshikawa (Eds.), *Changing schools and community organizations to foster positive youth development.* New York, NY: Oxford University Press.

Russell, S. T., Sinclair, K. O., Poteat, V. P., & Koenig, B. W. (2012). Adolescent health and harassment based on discriminatory bias. *American Journal of Public Health, 102,* 493–495.

Sawyer, A. L., Bradshaw, C. P., & O'Brennan, L. M. (2008). Examining ethnic, gender, and developmental differences in the way children report being a victim of "bullying" on self-report measures. *Journal of Adolescent Health, 43,* 106–114.

Turner, H. A., Finkelhor, D., Hamby, S. L., Shattuck, A., & Ormrod, R. K. (2011). Specifying type and location of peer victimization in a national sample of children and youth. *Journal of Youth and Adolescence, 40*(8), 1052–1067.

Wallace, T., Anderson, A. R., Bartholomay, T., & Hupp, S. (2002). An ecobehavioral examination of high school classrooms that include students with disabilities. *Exceptional Children, 68,* 345–359.

White, N. A., & Loeber, R. (2008). Bullying and special education as predictors of serious delinquency. *Journal of Research in Crime and Delinquency, 45,* 380–397. doi:10.1177/0022427808322612

Brief 4

Gender-Related Bullying
and Harassment:
A Growing Trend

Although research on bullying has grown since the 1970s, the research literature has generally ignored important influences related to gender and sexuality (Meyer, 2007). Bullying, sexual harassment, and homophobic and transphobic behaviors co-occur and need to be addressed to make schools safer and more inclusive. *Gendered harassment* is any unwanted behavior that enforces traditional, heterosexual gender norms. It is related to, and can overlap with, bullying. Forms of gendered harassment include sexual harassment; homophobic, biphobic, or transphobic harassment; and harassment for gender-nonconformity (Meyer, 2008, 2009).

State of the Knowledge

- The first study that used the same instruments to compare rates and impacts of bullying and sexual harassment showed that students experience high rates of both bullying (52%) and sexual harassment (34%) (Gruber & Fineran, 2008).

- Gay, lesbian, bisexual, and questioning students experienced more bullying (79% versus 50%) and more sexual harassment than heterosexual students (Coker, Austin,

Task Force members Elizabeth J. Meyer and V. Paul Poteat took the lead in drafting this brief.

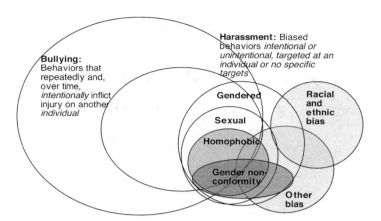

Forms of bullying and harassment (Meyer, 2009).

& Schuster, 2010; Gruber & Fineran, 2008; Poteat, Mereish, DiGiovanni, & Koenig, 2011).

- Both girls and boys experience sexual harassment (Hill & Kearl, 2011).

- Calling a student "gay" or "lesbian" is the one form of sexual harassment that has increased since 1993 (for boys, 9% in 1993, 19% in 2001 and 2011; for girls, 5% in 1993, 13% in 2001, 18% in 2011) (Harris Interactive, 2001; Hill & Kearl, 2011).

- Boys report increases in how frequently they are called gay epithets as they progress through high school (Poteat, O'Dwyer, & Mereish, 2012).

- Teachers are less likely to intervene in harassment related to sexual orientation, gender presentation, and body size than in that related to other forms of bias (race, religion, disability; California Safe Schools Coalition, 2004).

- Research indicates that students feel safer and report less harassment in schools where specific groups are listed as protected by anti-bullying laws and policies (Hatzenbuehler, 2011; Kosciw, Greytak, Diaz, & Bartkiewicz, 2010).

Legal Issues

The distinctions between bullying and harassment are important because they have different legal implications (see brief 5 for additional information). Gendered harassment must be addressed in accordance with federal guidelines that are part of Title IX. In October 2010, the U.S. Department of Education's Office for Civil Rights issued guidance to all school districts in the form of a "Dear Colleague" letter. In this letter there is clear wording regarding how Title IX applies in such cases:

> Title IX prohibits harassment of both male and female students regardless of the sex of the harasser—*i.e.*, even if the harasser and target are members of the same sex. It also prohibits gender-based harassment, which may include acts of verbal, non-verbal, or physical aggression, intimidation, or hostility based on sex or sex-stereotyping. Thus, it *can be sex discrimination if students are harassed either for exhibiting what is perceived as a stereotypical characteristic for their sex, or for failing to conform to stereotypical notions of masculinity and femininity.* Title IX also prohibits sexual harassment and gender-based harassment of all students, regardless of the actual or perceived sexual orientation or gender identity of the harasser or target. (Office for Civil Rights, U.S. Department of Education, 2010, pp. 7–8)

Conclusions and Implications

Studies make clear that awareness about gender-related bullying and broad-based knowledge of what is protected can increase students' sense of safety and student reports of less harassment. Policy and research implications follow from this knowledge.

Policy

- *Local:* School districts need to revise their bullying and harassment policies to explicitly include *all* forms of gendered harassment (sexual, sexual orientation, and gender identity/expression). Policies need to have clear implementation, reporting, and response mechanisms and align with federal laws, specifically Title IX. Educating staff, students, and families about policy revisions is an essential step for successful implementation.

- *Local:* Intervention programs need specifically to identify and teach about different forms of harassment and how these can be addressed along with general anti-bullying initiatives.

- *Federal:* Passage of federal bills that explicitly set forth specific groups covered under harassment, such as the Safe Schools Improvement Act (H.R. 1648) and the Student Non-Discrimination Act (H.R. 998), can have observable and meaningful benefits for the well-being of those vulnerable to gender-based harassment.

Research

- Survey items should allow for reporting forms of sexual, homophobic, gender-nonconforming, and transphobic harassment, as well as permit students to self-identify their gender identity (e.g., male, female, transgender, genderqueer, or other preferred gender identity) and sexual orientation (e.g., gay, lesbian, bisexual, queer, questioning, or other preferred sexual orientation identity). Inclusion of these items (e.g., sexual orientation as a demographic item and homophobic harassment indices) should constitute standard practice in bullying research, and analyses of these items should be reported in scholarly papers.

- Evaluation of anti-bullying programs should specifically track rates of different forms of harassment and staff interventions.

References

California Safe Schools Coalition & 4-H Center for Youth Development, University of California, Davis. (2004). *Consequences of harassment based on actual or perceived sexual orientation and gender non-conformity and steps to making schools safer.* San Francisco and Davis, CA: Authors.

Coker, T. R., Austin, S. B., & Schuster, M. A. (2010). The health and health care of lesbian, gay, and bisexual adolescents. *Annual Review of Public Health, 31,* 457–477.

Gruber, J. E., & Fineran, S. (2008). Comparing the impact of bullying and sexual harassment victimization on the mental and physical health of adolescents. *Sex Roles, 59,* 1–13.

Harris Interactive. (2001). *Hostile hallways: Bullying, teasing, and sexual harassment in school.* Washington, DC: American Association of University Women Educational Foundation.

Hatzenbuehler, M. L. (2011). The social environment and suicide attempts in lesbian, gay, and bisexual youth. *Pediatrics, 127*(5), 896–903.

Hill, C., & Kearl, H. (2011). *Crossing the line: Sexual harassment at school.* Washington, DC: American Association of University Women.

Kosciw, J., Greytak, E., Diaz, E. M., & Bartkiewicz, M. J. (2010). *2009 School Climate Survey: The experiences of lesbian, gay, bisexual and transgender youth in our nation's schools.* New York: GLSEN.

Meyer, E. J. (2007, April 9–13). *Bullying and harassment in secondary schools: A critical analysis of the gaps, overlaps, and implications from a decade of research.* Paper presented at the annual meeting of the American Educational Research Association, Chicago, IL.

Meyer, E. J. (2008). Gendered harassment in secondary schools: Understanding teachers' (non)interventions. *Gender and Education, 20*(6), 555–572.

Meyer, E. J. (2009). *Gender, bullying, and harassment: Strategies to end sexism and homophobia in schools.* New York: Teachers College Press.

Office for Civil Rights, U.S. Department of Education. (2010). "Dear Colleague" letter. Washington, DC: Author. Retrieved from http://www2.ed.gov/about/offices/list/ocr/letters/colleague-201010.html

Poteat, V. P., Mereish, E. H., DiGiovanni, C. D., & Koenig, B. W. (2011). The effects of general and homophobic victimization on adolescents' psychosocial and educational concerns: The importance of intersecting identities and parent support. *Journal of Counseling Psychology, 58*(4), 597–609.

Poteat, V. P., O'Dwyer, L. M., & Mereish, E. H. (2012). Changes in how students use and are called homophobic epithets over time: Patterns predicted by gender, bullying, and victimization status. *Journal of Educational Psychology, 104,* 393–406.

Brief 5

Legal Rights Related to Bullying and Discriminatory Harassment

Youth often express discrimination through behaviors typically labeled as bullying (Pascoe, 2007; Phoenix, Frosh, & Pattman, 2003). Failure to recognize that certain forms of bullying can constitute harassment can carry significant legal implications (Office for Civil Rights, U.S. Department of Education, 2010). Also, harassment based on one's social identity (e.g., gender, sexual orientation, race, religion), when compared with bullying, can have significantly more harmful mental health and social effects for targeted youth (Poteat, Mereish, DiGiovanni, & Koenig, 2011; Russell, Sinclair, Poteat, & Koenig, 2012).Thus, it is important for schools at all level to be vigilant about such behaviors, aware of the legal context, and transparent about their procedures for investigating and addressing such circumstances.

Determinations of Bullying and Harassment

When schools investigate potential bullying incidents, they should assess whether such incidents constitute harassment. Court decisions since *Davis v. Monroe County Board of Education* (1999) indicate that schools have an obligation to protect children from sexual harassment, and 49 states and the District of Columbia have laws requiring schools to address bul-

---

Task Force members V. Paul Poteat and Elizabeth J. Meyer took the lead in drafting this brief.

lying (Montana does not). Several implications follow from past cases and current legislation.

- Investigations by schools of possible harassment must be conducted expediently, thoroughly, and consistently.

- Schools should make known to students and parents specific procedures for reporting bullying and harassment, as well as whom to contact if cases are not handled expediently.

- Schools should advise students and parents of alternative reporting mechanisms (e.g., police) in cases of violence or other criminal activity.

- Schools should assess whether bullying experiences constitute a potential civil rights violation.

- Schools should be aware there is consistent evidence that zero-tolerance policies, originally applied to cases of school violence and weapon possession on campuses, but sometimes extended to bullying and harassment, are not effective.

- Knowledge of legal, procedural, and policy issues is central for schools in the effort to prevent bullying.

- Most legislation focuses on reporting, investigating, and intervening when bullying has occurred, but prevention efforts should be a key focus for school-based anti-bullying and harassment efforts.

Legislation at the State and Federal Levels

Many state anti-bullying laws also cover electronic forms of bullying and note the responsibilities of schools even when bullying occurs beyond school property. Policies vary in scope, definitions, mandates for training, and procedures for reporting, investigating, and intervening. And districts vary in how they implement these policies. Several resources provide overviews of state laws and pending legislation, including the 2011 U.S. Department of Education's *Analysis of State Bullying Laws and Policies* and a report by the Kinder and Braver World Project Research Series titled *An Overview of State Anti-Bullying Legislation and Other Related Laws* (Sacco, Silbaugh, Corredor, Casey, & Doherty, 2012). The National Association of State Boards of Education maintains a compilation of laws for each state.

When bullying behaviors constitute harassment or discrimination against a protected class (e.g., one defined by religion or race), the U.S. Department of Education Office of Civil Rights (OCR) and the U.S. Department of Justice Civil Rights Division may become involved. The Department of Health and Human Services maintains a website to educate the public about types of discriminatory behavior and the obligations of schools to address them (www.stopbullying.gov). When schools do not adequately address harassment, they may be in violation of civil rights laws, such as Title IV and Title VI of the Civil Rights Act of 1964; Title IX of the Education Amendments of 1972; Section 504 of the Rehabilitation Act of 1973; Titles II and III of the Americans with Disabilities Act; and the Individuals with Disabilities Education Act.

Although sexual orientation is not a protected class at the federal level at present, it is a protected class in certain state laws. The Student Non-Discrimination Act of 2011, currently under consideration, would extend federal protection against discrimination and harassment based on actual or perceived sexual orientation or gender identity.

Conclusions and Implications

Research is needed about how laws and legal policies related to bullying and harassment are understood or perceived. Also, little is known about how such policies affect students, whether victim or perpetrator. Understanding the impact and implementation of law and the role and relevance of a supportive legal context is fundamental to addressing bullying and harassment and making changes where necessary. Research should address such questions as:

- What components of anti-bullying policies actually produce reductions in bullying and harassment?

- How do educators, students, and parents perceive and react to these policies, and how does that affect the implementation and success of the policies?

- How do these policies and other systems-level factors operate in combination and with other individual-level factors to promote safer and more welcoming schools?

References

Office for Civil Rights, U.S. Department of Education. (2010). "Dear Colleague" letter. Washington, DC: Author. Retrieved from http://www2.ed.gov/about/offices/list/ocr/letters/colleague-201010.html

Pascoe, C. J. (2007). *Dude, you're a fag: Masculinity and sexuality in high school*. Berkeley, CA: University of California Press. Retrieved from http://search.proquest.com/docview/621521791?accountid=14553

Phoenix A., Frosh S., & Pattman R. (2003). Producing contradictory masculine subject positions: Narratives of threat, homophobia and bullying in 11–14 year old boys. *Journal of Social Issues, 59*(1), 179–195.

Poteat, V. P., Mereish, E. H., DiGiovanni, C. D., & Koenig, B. W. (2011). The effects of general and homophobic victimization on adolescents' psychosocial and educational concerns: The importance of intersecting identities and parent support. *Journal of Counseling Psychology, 58*(4), 597–609. doi:10.1037/a0025095

Russell, S. T., Sinclair, K. O., Poteat, V. P., & Koenig, B. W. (2012). Adolescent health and harassment based on discriminatory bias. *American Journal of Public Health, 102*(3), 493–495. doi:10.2105/AJPH.2011.300430

Sacco, D. T., Silbaugh, K., Corredor, F., Casey, J., & Doherty, D. (2012). *An overview of state anti-bullying legislation and other related laws* (The Kinder & Braver World Project: Research Series). Los Angeles, CA, and Cambridge, MA: Born This Way Foundation and Berkman Center for Internet & Society at Harvard University.

U.S. Department of Education. (2011). *Analysis of State Bullying Laws and Policies.* Washington, DC: Author.

Brief 6

Improving School Climate: A Critical Tool in Combating Bullying

Thousands of school climate surveys undertaken across America by the National School Climate Center (*Bully Prevention*, n.d.; *School Climate*, n.d.) consistently show a discrepancy between adult and student perceptions of school safety. Adults often report that school safety is a mild or moderate problem, while students often report that it is a severe problem.

Benefits of a Positive School Climate

School climate encompasses many factors, but there is substantial evidence that a positive school climate engages students in learning and promotes academic achievement and success. A study of 276 Virginia high schools found that a school climate characterized by lower rates of bullying and teasing was predictive of higher graduation rates four years later (Cornell, Gregory, Huang, & Fan, 2013). Schools with high levels of bullying and teasing had dropout rates 29% above the state average, compared with schools with a low level of bullying and teasing, which had a dropout rate 28% below average. The association between school climate and graduation rates was just as strong as the association between student poverty and graduation rates.

Task Force members Dewey Cornell and Dorothy L. Espelage took the lead in drafting this brief.

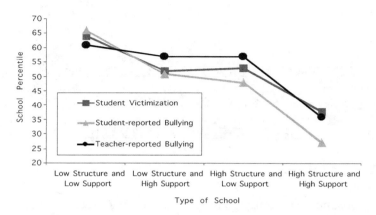

Victimization and bullying as a function of school structure and support.

Characteristics of Schools With Less Bullying

Schools with both fair discipline and a supportive atmosphere have less bullying. Research shows that high schools with an authoritative school climate, characterized by high levels of both disciplinary structure and adult support for students have lower levels of bullying and other forms of student victimization (Gregory, Cornell, Fan, Sheras, Shih, & Huang, 2010). High schools with low structure and low support had higher levels of bullying and other forms of student victimization (e.g., fights among peers, theft) that ranked them between the 60th and 66th percentiles among high schools, whereas high schools with high structure and high support had much lower levels of bullying and other student victimization (see figure).

Conclusions and Implications

A positive school climate is essential to bullying reduction and to student retention in school. There are research-based steps that educators can take to improve school climate, such as the following strategies:

- Develop a shared vision among educational leaders and the entire school community about what kind of school they want their school to be.

- Assess the school's strengths and needs in a comprehensive, reliable, and valid manner.

- Teach prosocial skills in regular classes, advisory classes, and other small-group experiences with opportunities for practice.

- Engage in prevention efforts that range from on-the-spot teaching with students who engage in teasing or bullying behavior to formal school-wide programs.

- Support partnerships among parents, educators, and mental health professionals who seek to interrupt the bully-victim-bystander cycle and encourage bystanders to be upstanders who do not allow bullying to continue.

References

Cornell, D., Gregory, A., Huang, F., & Fan, X. (2013). Perceived prevalence of bullying and teasing predicts high school dropout rates. *Journal of Educational Psychology, 105*(1), 138–149. doi:10.1037/a0030416

Gregory, A., Cornell, D., Fan, X., Sheras, P., Shih, T., & Huang, F. (2010). Authoritative school discipline: High school practices associated with lower student bullying and victimization. *Journal of Educational Psychology, 102*, 483–496.

National School Climate Center. (n.d.). *Bully prevention.* New York: Author. Retrieved from https://schoolclimate.org/prevention

National School Climate Center. (n.d.). *School Climate.* New York: Author. Retrieved from http://www.schoolclimate.org/climate

Brief 7

Students, Teachers, Support Staff, Administrators, and Parents Working Together to Prevent and Reduce Bullying

School personnel and bystander students can make a significant difference in rates of bullying. Schools where staff, parents, and students create common norms and ways of dealing with bullying can achieve sustainable reductions in victimization.

Identifying the Need for Comprehensive Prevention Programs

There is a compelling need for schools to strengthen their delivery of social-behavioral prevention programs to achieve a well-coordinated, efficient, and comprehensive school-wide approach (Mayer & Furlong, 2010).

- Theory and applied research have repeatedly stressed the importance of involving the individual, peer groups, school, family, and the community in preventing bullying (Benbenishty & Astor, 2005).

- Research has established that bullying is a social phenomenon that goes beyond the bully-victim interaction and depends greatly on peer group dynamics and the

---

Task Force members Ron Avi Astor and Matthew J. Mayer took the lead in drafting this brief.

critical role of bystanders (Benbenishty & Astor, 2012; Espelage, 2012).

Taking a Diversified Intervention Approach in Concert With Bullying Programs

- Social and emotional learning can help students become more respectful and considerate of others (Espelage & Low, 2012).

- There is a range of universal and more focused interventions that can improve student behavior (Ttofi & Farrington, 2011).

- Studies have identified more effective discipline practices and determined that the widespread emphasis on school suspension is ineffective (American Psychological Association Zero Tolerance Task Force, 2008; Durlak, Weissberg, Dymnicki, Taylor, & Schellinger, 2011).

Targeting Social Dynamic Change in Hot-Spot Locations and Times

While some bullying occurs in classrooms, most occurs in situations involving a large proportion of students and few or no school staff members, for example in the hallways during transitions, on playgrounds and routes to and from schools, and in buses, restrooms, and cafeterias.

- School efforts must focus on a wide array of peer group contexts, with particular attention to empowering peer and staff bystanders to prevent bullying.

- It is possible to greatly reduce bullying by directly addressing bystander peer norms, behaviors, and dynamics so that peers deter bullies, support victims, recognize the harm they may cause with rumors or gossiping, and are committed to reporting severe acts to teachers or administrators (Astor, Benbenishty & Estrada, 2009).

- The peer group and staff witnessing bullying events need to be trained in how to respond in hot-spot locations (Astor, Meyer, & Behre, 1999). A wide array of school support staff, including bus monitors, security personnel, cafeteria workers, janitorial workers, secretaries, and substitute teachers can also contribute to bullying reduction.

Conclusions and Implications

Schools and communities should consider a well-coordinated approach to developing strong home-school partnerships, coupled with wider community-level efforts to teach young people appropriate social-emotional skills, concern for others, and an appreciation for civility, which are essential to the well-being of our society. School, parent, and community stakeholders can work together to significantly lower rates of bullying. Necessary actions to promote such change include the following (Astor, Guerra, & Van Acker, 2010):

- Create a "living" and dynamic school policy on bullying that all embrace;

- Provide training for students, staff, and parents on creating common norms and ways to deal with bullying incidents;

- Emphasize the social and emotional mission of the school in communications with all constituents and integrate it into the curriculum;

- Create and maintain open lines of communication to report and respond to incidents;

- Facilitate opportunities for staff, students, and parents to discuss the topic and its solutions across academic and social contexts;

- Address mental health needs linked to persistent or extreme bullying situations;

- Educate and involve parents and other community members in the identification of bullying behaviors and responses that reduce such behaviors; and

- Establish clear and developmentally appropriate consequences for peer groups that encourage or instigate bullying behaviors.

Bridging the research-to-practice gap, scholars can provide resources to help stakeholders to:

- Empower bystanders to prevent bullying;

- Change peer-group and school staff norms regarding bystander behavior;

- Respond more efficiently to the local cultural context;

- Create next-generation approaches to meet the specific needs of school communities (e.g., combining elements of Social-Emotional Learning and School-wide Positive Behavioral Supports); and

- Improve efficiency of prevention and intervention approaches (www.stopbullying.gov).

References

American Psychological Association Zero Tolerance Task Force. (2008). Are zero tolerance policies effective in the schools? An evidentiary review and recommendations. *American Psychologist, 63,* 852–862.

Astor, R. A., Benbenishty, R., & Estrada, J. (2009). School violence and theoretically atypical schools: The principal's centrality in orchestrating safe schools. *American Educational Research Journal, 46(2),* 423–461.

Astor, R. A., Meyer, H., & Behre, W. J. (1999). Unowned places and times: Maps and interviews about violence in high schools. *American Educational Research Journal, 36,* 3–42

Astor, R.A., Guerra, N., & Van Acker, R. (2010). How can we improve school safety research? *Educational Researcher, 39,* 69–78.

Benbenishty, R., & Astor, R. A. (2005). *School violence in context: Culture, neighborhood, family, school, and gender.* New York: Oxford University Press.

Benbenishty, R., & Astor, R. A. (2012). Monitoring school violence in Israel, national studies and beyond: Implications for theory, practice, and policy. In S. R. Jimerson, A. B. Nickerson, M. J. Mayer & M. J. Furlong (Eds), *Handbook of school violence and school safety: International research and practice* (2nd ed., pp. 191–202). New York: Routledge.

Durlak, J. A., Weissberg, R. P., Dymnicki, A. B., Taylor, R. D., & Schellinger, K. B. (2011). The impact of enhancing students' social and emotional learning: A meta-analysis of school-based universal interventions. *Child Development, 82,* 405–432.

Espelage, D. L. (2012). Bullying prevention: A research dialogue with Dorothy Espelage. *Prevention Researcher, 19(3),* 17–19.

Espelage, D., & Low, S. M. (2012). Bullying among children and adolescents: Social-emotional learning approaches to prevention. In K. Nader (Ed.), *School rampage shootings and other youth disturbances: Early preventative interventions* (pp. 205–219). New York: Routledge.

Mayer, M. J., & Furlong, M. J. (2010). How safe are our schools? *Educational Researcher, 39,* 16–26.

Ttofi, M. M., & Farrington, D. P. (2011). Effectiveness of school-based programs to reduce bullying: A systematic review and meta-analytic review. *Journal of Experimental Criminology, 7,* 27–56. doi:10.1007/s11292-010-9109-1

Brief 8

Bullying and Harassment on College Campuses: Misunderstood and Underaddressed

Bullying and harassment in various forms are familiar aspects of higher education settings. The victims and perpetrators include multiple constituent groups: university employees, including faculty, administrators, and staff; and students, whose bullying and harassment experiences are qualitatively different from those of their paid counterparts.

Bullying in higher education is different from that in K–12 educational settings and other organizations. Higher education institutions have a diverse set of employee contracts, for part-time and full-time faculty, professional staff, nonprofessional staff, administrators, and student employees (graduate assistants, for example). The presence of varying types of employees alongside tuition-paying students results in unique power dynamics, which, in turn, lead to complexity regarding who is defined as victim or perpetrator; for example, students may bully or harass faculty despite faculty's relative power in the institutional hierarchy. Colleges and universities also have unique structural aspects, such as tenure, that play a role in how bullying occurs.

Task Force members Jaime Lester and Elizabeth J. Meyer took the lead in drafting this brief.

University Employees and Their Experiences With Bullying

While specific forms of harassment (i.e., sexual harassment) and discrimination have a strong empirical record and legal protections under Title IX, Title VII of the Civil Rights Act of 1964, and the Age Discrimination in Employment Act of 1967, university workplace bullying has only recently received attention by researchers. Studies reveal that:

- The rates of bullying among faculty and staff range from 32% to 52% in the United States and Canada (McKay, Arnold, Fratzl, & Thomas, 2008).

- Among university employees, the victim-to-perpetrator relationship is strongly influenced by organizational structure. Faculty members are more likely to be bullied by other faculty, and academic managers are likely to be bullied by frontline staff (Keashly & Neuman, 2008).

- The duration of bullying among faculty and staff typically is three to more than five years (Hoel, Einarsen, & Cooper, 2003).

- Workplace bullying, defined as bullying among employees, including faculty and staff, has a broad impact, including the following (Hoel, Einarsen, & Cooper, 2003):

- Reducing organizational learning and creativity

- Imperiling financial efficiency by reducing productivity

- Creating an unhealthy and revolving workforce that reduces student retention and success

- In extreme and rare cases, acting as a precursor to violence

University Students and
Their Experiences With Bullying

Among students in colleges and universities, bullying and harassment take the form of sexual harassment, hazing, violence, and cyberbullying. Robust national studies indicate that:

- 70% of students who have been bullied in elementary or high school are also bullied in college (Chapell et al., 2006).

- 62% of female college students and 61% of male college students report having been sexually harassed at their university (Hill & Silva, 2006).

- 55% of students involved in clubs, teams, and organizations experience hazing (Allan & Madden, 2008).

New types of bullying, such as cyberbullying, are only beginning to emerge in the research:

- One study found that 11% of students have experienced cyberbullying at college (Walker, Sockman, & Koehn, 2011).

- More than half of hazing incidents among college students result in public pictures on the Internet.

Bullying in higher education among students cannot be ignored. A 2008 national study of hazing in college (Allan & Madden, 2008) found that:

- The vast majority (95%) of students did not report hazing to campus officials.

- Hazing occurs across a variety of student activities, including but not limited to Greek-letter organizations, student groups, athletics, and honors clubs.

- Students report limited exposure to hazing prevention programs on college campuses.

Neglect of Bullying in Higher Education

Several major issues complicate the understanding of bullying and harassment in higher education, including the lack of clear definitions, the structural differentiation of the academic environment, and localized social and cultural norms that accept, or even reinforce, bullying.

- Structurally and culturally separate units across college campuses use different terms (*incivility, harassment, hazing, bullying,* etc.), definitions, and techniques to address bullying.

- Human resource departments and ombudsmen may use mediators to address bullying among faculty and staff, while judicial review committees apply specific sanctions (i.e., suspension or expulsion) for students who bully or harass their peers. Fraternities and sororities also have separate anti-hazing policies and various accountability mechanisms that are external to universities. Coordination across these internal and external units is limited.

- Colleges and universities have limited legal standing to address bullying that does not involve a legally protected category or documented threats of violence.

There is an absence of systematic research on bullying in higher education:

- The research on workplace bullying among staff and faculty has used varying definitions of bullying, focused on campus case studies, and relied on small samples that do not provide comparative statistics.

- Only a few studies in the past 15 years have tracked the prevalence of bullying among university employees in higher education, and their findings vary widely, from approximately 30% to 50%. There is a need for data about the prevalence and nature of bullying and harassment among university employees in higher education and how these behaviors differ across institutional types (i.e., community colleges, public universities, and private liberal arts colleges).

- Studies that include university employees as well as students are limited primarily to dated research on student course evaluations and behaviors in classroom settings. Little is known about the potential cumulative cultural impact of bullying and harassment across constituent groups on college campuses.

Conclusions and Implications

Research has begun to shed light on how the structure and context of academe can promote bullying and harassment behaviors (Twale & DeLuca, 2008), but much more needs to be done to understand how often these behaviors occur, why they occur, and the effective means to combat their prevalence on campus. Future research to address the gaps in knowledge should include:

- *A national study of bullying and harassment in higher education that includes students, faculty, and staff.* This study would provide the data that national and state policy makers and individual institutional leaders need to understand the necessity of addressing bullying and harassment behaviors beyond the existing protected-category legislation in Title IX. The study could include sexual harassment and assault but would also move beyond protected categories to address bullying behaviors that do not fall under Title IX legislation. The data could serve as a call for anti-bullying legislation to extend beyond the K–12 system to include higher education institutions.

- *Institutional research that systematically examines bullying and harassment on campuses.* The data from this research could be used to promote anti-bullying cultures through honor codes and civility campaigns addressing all campus constituent groups: faculty, staff, leaders, and students.

Such research could help foster clear, evidence-based policies that cut across institutional structural silos separating groups within higher education that play a role in the prevention of bullying and harassment (such as college departments; offices of student affairs, of academic affairs, of equity and diversity; and fraternities and sororities). Such research can also contribute to a national conversation across higher education associations, research associations, federal agencies, and private foundations about the conditions in higher education that foster bullying and harassment and steps that can be taken to reduce risk and lead to better prevention. Training on bullying separate from or in addition to training on sexual harassment, and campus-wide campaigns to educate campus communities on the legal, ethical, cultural, and policy implications of bullying, could follow from such efforts.

References

Allan, E., & Madden, M. (2008). *Hazing in view: College students at risk. Initial findings from the National Study of Student Hazing.* Orono, ME: National Collaborative for Hazing Research and Prevention. Retrieved from http://www.hazingstudy.org

Chapell, M., Casey, D., De la Cruz, C., Ferrell, J., Forman, J. L. R., Newsham, M., Sterling, M., & Whitaker, S. (2006). Bullying in university by students and teachers. *Adolescence, 39,* 53–64.

Hill, C., & Silva, E. (2006). *Drawing the line: Sexual harassment on campus.* Washington, DC: American Association of University Women.

Hoel, H., Einarsen, S., & Cooper, C. L. (2003). Organizational effects of bullying. In S. Einarsen, H. Hoel, D. Zapf, & C. L. Cooper (Eds.), *Bullying and emotional abuse in the workplace: International perspectives in research and practice* (pp. 145–161). London: Taylor & Francis.

Keashly, L., & Neuman, J. H. (2008). *Final report: Workplace Behavior (Bullying) Project Survey.* Mankato, MN: Minnesota State University.

McKay, R., Arnold, D. H., Fratzl, J., & Thomas, R. (2008). Workplace bullying in academia: A Canadian study. *Employee Responsibilities and Rights Journal, 20,* 77–100.

Twale, D. J., & DeLuca, B. M. (2008). *Faculty incivility: The rise of the academic bully culture and what to do about it.* San Francisco, CA: Jossey-Bass.

Walker, C. M., Sockman, B. R., & Koehn, S. (2011). An exploratory study of cyberbullying with undergraduate university students. *Tech Trends,* 55(2), 31–38.

Brief 9

Using Evidence-Based Programs in Schools to Take on Bullying

Bullying often goes undetected by adults. Bullying can cover a wide array of actions, such as name-calling, sexual harassment, hate crimes, weapon threats, social exclusion, and public humiliation. These diverse forms of bullying may require different intervention approaches (Benbenishty & Astor, 2005). That is why assessment strategies for recognizing potential problems (listed below) are so vital.

Anti-bullying programs should begin with a schoolwide assessment of how much bullying is taking place, followed by the implementation of an evidence-based program. Schools should regularly monitor their level of bullying to make sure their anti-bullying efforts are effective.

How Should Schools Assess Bullying?

- Surveys and focus groups with students are a good way to begin when assessing the nature and extent of peer victimization in a school. This baseline assessment can raise awareness of bullying, as well as provide a benchmark for measuring progress after a program is initiated.

Task Force members Ron Avi Astor and Dewey Cornell took the lead in drafting this brief.

- Schools should use reliable and valid surveys (http:// stacks.cdc.gov/view/cdc/5994) rather than create their own.

- Focus groups can be used to gather multiple perspectives about student needs and school policies and practices.

- Information collected from students should be supplemented with other sources of information, such as staff observations and surveys, disciplinary records, and parent perceptions.

What Kinds of Information Should Be Collected?

- Who is being bullied? What groups are being targeted (e.g., by age, gender, ethnicity, language, sexual orientation, or social cliques)?

- When and where is bullying taking place (Astor, Meyer, & Behre, 1999)?

- How are students and staff members responding to bullying events?

- Does the overall school climate prevent bullying (Gregory, Cornell, & Fan, 2011)? For example, do students feel supported and respected by teachers, and are they willing to seek help for bullying? Do students regard school discipline as strict but fair?

How Should Schools Use Their Assessment Results?

- Feedback to the school community sends a strong message of concern that can help change the school culture.

- The presentation of results to groups of stakeholders can elicit dialogue and exchange of views leading to consensus and a plan of action.

- A careful and comprehensive assessment will help match school needs with appropriate evidence-based programs. (All the recommendations in this section are from Benbenishty & Astor, 2012.)

Why Use an Evidence-Based Program?

It is not easy to reduce bullying. Many programs marketed to schools are not supported by scientific evidence of effectiveness. A program that seems compelling may nevertheless have no sustained impact on student behavior. An evidence-based program, on the other hand, has a certain amount of research supporting its effectiveness in school settings.

How Should Schools Select an Evidence-Based Program?

There are good resources to identify anti-bullying programs that have been rigorously tested and found to be effective. Among them are the National Registry of Evidence-based Programs and Practices (http://www.nrepp.samhsa.gov/), Blueprints for Healthy Youth Development (http://www.colorado.edu/cspv/blueprints/), and the Model Programs Guide (http://www.ojjdp.gov/mpg/).

Important Points to Consider in Selecting an Evidence-Based Program

- Evidence-based programs vary in effectiveness.

- They are designed for different student populations (e.g., different age groups and racial/ethnic populations) and different forms of bullying.

- No evidence-based program is likely to be effective without high-quality implementation (Astor, Guerra, & Van Acker, 2010).

References

Astor, R. A., Guerra, N., & Van Acker, R. (2010). How can we improve school safety research? *Educational Researcher, 39,* 69–78.

Astor, R. A., Meyer, H., & Behre, W. J. (1999). Unowned places and times: Maps and interviews about violence in high schools. *American Educational Research Journal, 36,* 3–42.

Benbensihty, R., & Astor, R. A. (2005). *School violence in context: Culture, neighborhood, family, school, and gender.* New York: Oxford University Press.

Benbenishty, R., & Astor, R. A. (2012). Monitoring school violence in Israel, national studies and beyond: Implications for theory, practice, and policy. In S. R. Jimerson, A. B. Nickerson, M. J. Mayer, & M. J. Furlong (Eds.), *Handbook of school violence and school safety: International research and practice* (2nd ed., pp.191–202). New York: Routledge.

Gregory, A., Cornell, D., & Fan, X. (2011). The relationship of school structure and support to suspension rates for Black and White high school students. *American Educational Research Journal, 48,* 904–934.

Brief 10

Putting School Safety Education at the Core of Professional Preparation Programs

University schools of education and social work, as well as administrator preparation programs at the principal and superintendent levels, should integrate instruction in harassment, intimidation, and bullying (HIB) prevention and school safety education into their preservice and preparation programs for K–12 education, which include degree curricula, certification training programs, and continuing education programs.

Assessing Prevention Training Needs

Virtually all states have enacted school bullying prevention laws, and most state laws require some form of bullying prevention training for teachers, administrators, and allied professional staff (Bradshaw, Waasdorp, O'Brennan, Gulemetova, & Henderson, 2011).

The laws, while important for acknowledging the role of training and school climate in HIB prevention, place the responsibility of developing training on individual schools or school districts, some of which have limited knowledge of HIB prevention. These mandates are often unfunded, requiring schools and school districts to find sufficient funds to establish training programs and evaluation mechanisms.

Task Force members Jaime Lester and Matthew J. Mayer took the lead in drafting this brief.

59

- A recent national study found that only half of school employees—professional staff and teachers—had received training related to a bullying prevention policy, and over half of all teachers and professional staff felt a need for additional HIB training (Bradshaw et al., 2011).

- School teachers and staff have demonstrated perceptions that are strikingly different from the perceptions of students regarding student bullying victimization experiences in school (e.g., 58% of students versus 25% of teachers and staff reported that students push, shove, or trip weaker students) (Low, Brown, & Smith, 2011).

- Communication between students and school personnel about bullying incidents is problematic. Among students between the ages of 12 and 18 in 2009, only 36% who reported being bullied at school had notified an adult at school (Robers, Zhang, Truman, Snyder, 2012).

Serious disconnects exist in schools with regard to bullying in the areas of accurate perception of environment, functional communication between students and staff, and training. This situation points to an unmet need for preservice university training on HIB prevention for future teachers, administrators, and school social workers. Colleges and universities—primary sources of professional training and knowledge dissemination—should integrate bullying prevention into curricula to meet this need.

Taking a Balanced Approach

HIB training programs at the university level need to balance the following:

- Leveraging the empirical research base

- Establishing key focus areas in training, such as the prevalence of bullying, social-psychological factors linked to bullying, harm resulting from school violence and HIB, approaches to data collection and analysis, approaches to prevention, roles of professionals, integration of bullying prevention with existing school programming, extension of bullying prevention beyond the school to the local community, and state-specific training on state bullying laws and local context

- Ensuring adequate distributed training across and within specific courses, avoiding a mass training approach (e.g., all-day workshops)

- Linking appropriately to established major programmatic approaches (e.g., School-wide Positive Behavior Support and Social-Emotional Learning) and major bullying prevention packages (e.g., Steps to Respect) for fostering research-to-practice connections

- Examining approaches to continuing professional development for practitioners

Conclusions and Implications

There is considerable value to building on research and the knowledge of experts in devising professional development programs. One cost-effective approach is to convene relevant stakeholders to produce a guidance document. A national panel that includes representatives from major professional groups in education research, psychology, counseling, and social work (e.g., the American Educational Research Association, the American Psychological Association, the National Association of Student Personnel Administrators, and the National Association of Social Workers); from university training programs; from accreditation agencies (e.g., the Council for the Accreditation of Educator Preparation), and from other key stakeholders would be well situated to develop and disseminate a national-level guidance document. Also, representatives from major federal agencies, including the Departments of Education, Justice, and Health and Human

Services, should be included. A guidance document should include specific recommendations for school safety and HIB-related university training of preservice personnel preparing to work in schools and related educational settings.

References

Bradshaw, C. P., Waasdorp, T. E., O'Brennan, L. M., Gulemetova, M., & Henderson, R. D. (2011). *Findings from the National Education Association's nationwide study of bullying: Teachers' and education support professionals' perspectives.* Washington, DC: National Education Association.

Low, S., Brown, E., & Smith, B. (2011). Design and analysis of a randomized controlled trial of Steps to Respect. *Bullying in North American schools.* New York: Routledge.

Robers, S., Zhang, J., Truman, J., & Snyder, T. (2012). *Indicators of school crime and safety: 2011* (NCES 2012-002/NCJ 236021). Washington, DC: National Center for Education Statistics, U.S. Department of Education, and Bureau of Justice Statistics, Office of Justice Programs, U.S. Department of Justice.

Brief 11

Reinvigorated Data Collection and Analysis: A Charge for National and Federal Stakeholders

More rigorous, standardized, and efficient measures of school climate and bullying are needed to monitor and improve school conditions in K–16 settings. National safety programs and federal agencies should come to an agreement about which data collection approaches to use with bullying prevention. Common data standards and measures are important so that state and national surveillance systems can track progress effectively over time.

Assessing the Current Situation

Current national assessments and data collection methods constitute a fragmented approach.

- There are varying definitional and measurement approaches to constructs such as bullying.

- Prevention and intervention policies and programs require use of a common language to consistently measure and analyze variables of interest and for cohesive program evaluation.

Task Force members Matthew J. Mayer and V. Paul Poteat took the lead in drafting this brief.

Key areas of bullying prevention require further study, including:

- Bystander behaviors
- Group norms
- Social-organizational factors (e.g., inadequate teacher training)
- Interactions across settings and situations

Research is needed to better adapt interventions to unique needs across schools.

Taking a Broad and Multilayered Approach

Multiple school climate models and measurement approaches are currently under study. Researchers, policy makers, and practitioners need to base their work and policies on well-conceived models of school climate and school safety.

- Specific attention should be given to factors such as bystander behaviors, group norms, systemic organizational factors (e.g., teacher training), and risk and protective factors.

- Federal and state agencies should fund and support technical assistance centers to provide organizations with current knowledge, strategies, and tools for successfully implementing prevention and intervention programs.

Conclusions and Implications

States, school districts, and schools should employ scientifically sound instruments and seek expert guidance about their proper use at the local level. Also, there needs to be increased research support from federal funding agencies for longitudinal and experimental studies. In addition, basic research on the causes of bullying and harassment should receive greater attention in setting R&D priorities. Investing resources in data collection and the production of useful knowledge is, in the long run, key to understanding and reducing bullying and enhancing school climate.

Suggested Readings

Astor, R. A., Guerra, N. G., & Van Acker, R. (2010). How can we improve school safety research? *Educational Researcher, 39*, 68–79.

Espelage, D. L., & Holt, M. K. (2012). Understanding and preventing bullying and sexual harassment in school. In K. R. Harris, S. Graham, T. Urdan, S. Graham, J. M. Royer, & M. Zeidner (Eds.), *APA educational psychology handbook, Vol 2. Individual differences and cultural and contextual factors* (pp. 391–416). Washington, DC: American Psychological Association.

Espelage, D. L., & Poteat, V. P. (2012). School-based prevention of peer relationship problems. In B. Altmaier & J. Hansen (Eds.), *The Oxford handbook of counseling psychology* (pp.703–722). New York: Oxford University Press.

Espelage, D. L., & Swearer, S. M. (Eds.). (2011). *Bullying in North American schools* (2nd ed.). New York: Routledge.

Jimerson, S. R., Swearer, S. M., & Espelage, D. L. (Eds.). (2010). *The handbook of bullying in schools: An international perspective.* New York: Routledge.

Mayer, M. J., & Furlong, M. J. (2010). How safe are our schools? *Educational Researcher, 39*, 16–26.

Biographical Sketches of
AERA Task Force Members

Co-Chairs

Dorothy L. Espelage is a Professor in the Department of Educational Psychology at the University of Illinois, Urbana-Champaign. She has conducted research on bullying, homophobic teasing, sexual harassment, and dating violence for the last 20 years. She has more than 100 research publications and four books. Espelage is Associate Editor of the *Journal of Counseling Psychology* and 2010–2013 Vice-President of AERA's Division E. She is Principal Investigator on a Centers for Disease Control–funded randomized clinical trial of a prevention program in 36 middle schools to reduce bullying and sexual violence. The National Science Foundation has funded her work to develop better observational methods to assess bullying among adolescents. The National Institute of Justice is funding a longitudinal study on bullying and dating violence among adolescents, and Espelage serves as co-Principal Investigator on that study with RAND colleagues.

Ron Avi Astor is the Thor Professor in Urban Social Development at the University of Southern California School of Social Work and Rossier School of Education. His research documents the ecological influences of family, community, school, and culture on school violence. With colleagues he has authored more than 150 scientific publications. An AERA fellow, Astor is also a recipient of AERA's Palmer O. Johnson Memorial Award and Outstanding Book Award (*School Violence in Context*, Oxford University Press). From AERA's Division E he twice received the Distinguished Research Award, and from its Conflict Resolution SIG, the Promise Award. Astor is currently working to improve school safety in public schools that have large numbers of military students. Four of his guides for educators, counselors, administrators, and parents in public, military-connected schools were recently published by Teachers College Press.

Members

Dewey Cornell is the Bunker Professor of Education in the Curry School of Education at the University of Virginia. He directs the Virginia Youth Violence Project and serves as a program director for Youth-Nex, the Center to Promote Effective Youth Development. His interest in bullying grew from work as a forensic clinical psychologist, where he observed that bullying played a substantial role in several school shootings. His research includes the development of the Virginia Student Threat Assessment Guidelines, which provides schools with an effective alternative to zero tolerance disciplinary practices. He is currently directing a National Institute of Justice–funded statewide assessment of school climate and bullying in more than 700 Virginia secondary schools.

Jaime Lester is an Associate Professor of Higher Education at George Mason University. Her research applies organizational and feminist theories to examine inequitable workplace practice in colleges and universities. She has received numerous awards from national associations for her research and teaching and has over 50 publications. She also has had four books on gendered perspectives in community colleges, family-friendly policies in higher education, ways to restructure higher education to promote collaboration, and grassroots leadership for organizational change published by Stanford University Press. Her latest book is on workplace bullying in higher education. Lester received her Ph.D. and M.Ed. in higher education from the Rossier School of Education at the University of Southern California. She also holds a dual B.A. from the University of Michigan in English and women's studies.

Matthew J. Mayer is a Professor and the Coordinator of Special Education Programs in the Graduate School of Education at Rutgers University. Before entering higher education, Mayer was a special education teacher, with several years of educational case management work in foster care and educational outreach with at-risk children. He has published on school violence prevention, cognitive-behavioral interventions, and methodological issues in evidence-based research. Mayer is on the editorial boards of *Behavioral Disorders, School Psychology Quarterly,* and the *Journal of School Violence* and is coeditor of the *Handbook of School Violence and School Safety* (2nd ed.). In addition to his research, Mayer maintains an active agenda of graduate-level training, addressing special education topics and issues such as racial disproportionality in special education classification and student discipline.

Elizabeth J. Meyer is an Assistant Professor in the School of Education at California Polytechnic State University in San Luis Obispo. She is the author of *Gender, Bullying, and Harassment: Strategies to End Sexism and Homophobia in Schools* (Teachers College Press, 2009) and *Gender and Sexual Diversity in Schools* (Springer, 2010). She is a former high school teacher and Fulbright Teacher Exchange Program grantee. Meyer completed her M.A. at the University of Colorado, Boulder, and her Ph.D. at McGill University in Montreal, Quebec. Her research has been published in academic journals such as *Gender and Education,* the *McGill Journal of Education, The Clearinghouse, Computers and Education,* and the *Journal of LGBT Youth.* She blogs for *Psychology Today* and is also on Twitter: @lizjmeyer.

V. Paul Poteat is an Assistant Professor in the Department of Counseling, Developmental, and Educational Psychology at Boston College. His research examines individual attributes and broader peer group norms that contribute to engagement in homophobic bullying, as well as the mental health outcomes and resilience of youth who are targets of this form of victimization. He has published over 40 papers on bullying, prejudice, and systems of oppression across the fields of developmental, social, counseling, and educational psychology. Recently, he received funding to identify components of gay-straight alliances that contribute to healthy development among LGBT youth. He has also received funding to examine bias in exclusionary and punitive discipline (e.g., suspension) against LGBT youth and the mechanisms by which this occurs. His work has been used to inform school-based protective policies for LGBT youth and youth from other marginalized populations.

Brendesha Tynes is an Associate Professor of Education and Psychology at the University of Southern California Rossier School of Education. Her research focuses on online victimization and meeting adolescents' developmental needs in blended learning environments. She is the principal investigator of a National Institutes of Health–funded longitudinal study of online racial discrimination and its impact on academic performance, mental health, and behavior. Tynes received her Ph.D. from the University of California, Los Angeles, and was a research fellow in the Department of Society, Human Development and Health at Harvard University. Her awards include the 2012 AERA

Early Career Award for significant scholarly contributions to issues affecting minority populations. She has been quoted on bullying and new media–related issues in the *New York Times*, the *Los Angeles Times*, the *Huffington Post*, and on CNN and numerous other outlets.